Alexander Marshal's Nature Coloring Book

Drawings from the
The Royal Collection

SIRIUS

The Royal Collection

The Royal Collection is among the largest and most important art collections in the world, and one of the last great European royal collections to remain intact. A department of the Royal Household, Royal Collection Trust is responsible for the care of the Royal Collection and manages the public opening of the official residences of The King. Income generated from admissions and from associated commercial activities contributes directly to the Royal Collection Trust, a registered charity. Explore the Royal Collection at www.rct.uk.

Publishers' Note

The names of the plants shown on pages 4–7 are the original ones as written down by Alexander Marshal. They are not necessarily the names by which these plants are now known.

SIRIUS

This edition published in 2024 by Sirius Publishing, a division of Arcturus Publishing Limited,
26/27 Bickels Yard, 151–153 Bermondsey Street,
London SE1 3HA

Copyright © Arcturus Holdings Limited

ISBN: 978-1-3988-4451-3
CH011167NT

Printed in China

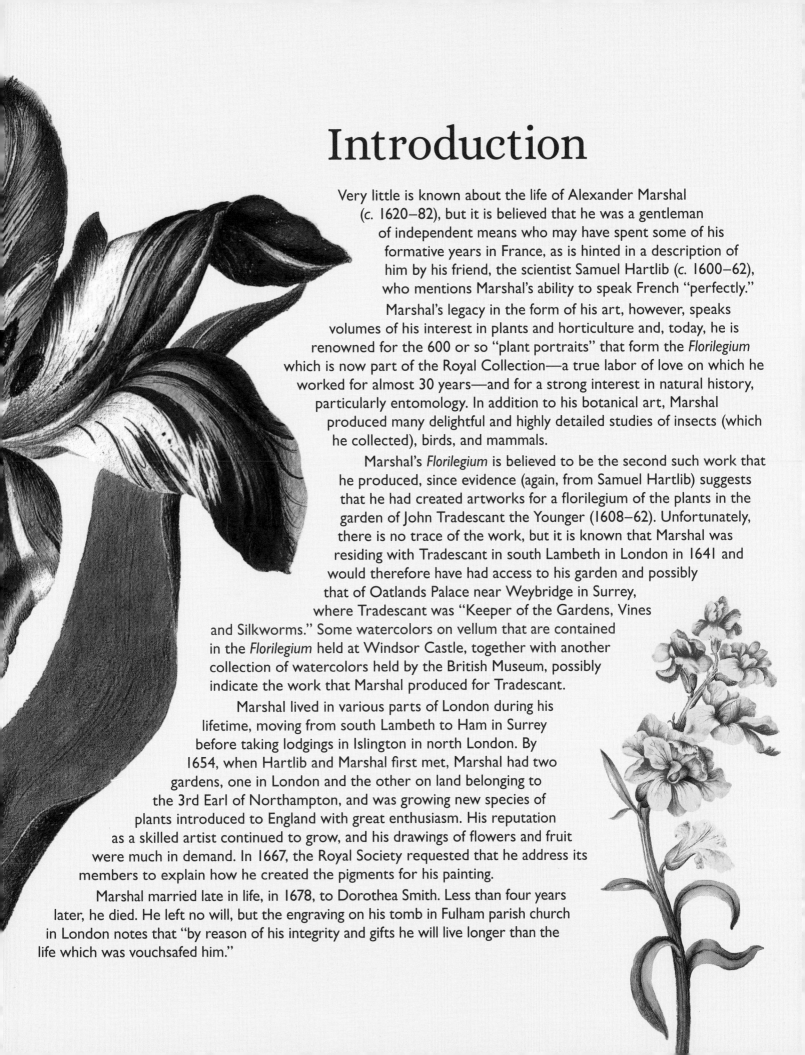

Introduction

Very little is known about the life of Alexander Marshal (c. 1620–82), but it is believed that he was a gentleman of independent means who may have spent some of his formative years in France, as is hinted in a description of him by his friend, the scientist Samuel Hartlib (c. 1600–62), who mentions Marshal's ability to speak French "perfectly."

Marshal's legacy in the form of his art, however, speaks volumes of his interest in plants and horticulture and, today, he is renowned for the 600 or so "plant portraits" that form the *Florilegium* which is now part of the Royal Collection—a true labor of love on which he worked for almost 30 years—and for a strong interest in natural history, particularly entomology. In addition to his botanical art, Marshal produced many delightful and highly detailed studies of insects (which he collected), birds, and mammals.

Marshal's *Florilegium* is believed to be the second such work that he produced, since evidence (again, from Samuel Hartlib) suggests that he had created artworks for a florilegium of the plants in the garden of John Tradescant the Younger (1608–62). Unfortunately, there is no trace of the work, but it is known that Marshal was residing with Tradescant in south Lambeth in London in 1641 and would therefore have had access to his garden and possibly that of Oatlands Palace near Weybridge in Surrey, where Tradescant was "Keeper of the Gardens, Vines and Silkworms." Some watercolors on vellum that are contained in the *Florilegium* held at Windsor Castle, together with another collection of watercolors held by the British Museum, possibly indicate the work that Marshal produced for Tradescant.

Marshal lived in various parts of London during his lifetime, moving from south Lambeth to Ham in Surrey before taking lodgings in Islington in north London. By 1654, when Hartlib and Marshal first met, Marshal had two gardens, one in London and the other on land belonging to the 3rd Earl of Northampton, and was growing new species of plants introduced to England with great enthusiasm. His reputation as a skilled artist continued to grow, and his drawings of flowers and fruit were much in demand. In 1667, the Royal Society requested that he address its members to explain how he created the pigments for his painting.

Marshal married late in life, in 1678, to Dorothea Smith. Less than four years later, he died. He left no will, but the engraving on his tomb in Fulham parish church in London notes that "by reason of his integrity and gifts he will live longer than the life which was vouchsafed him."

Six *Primula* x *pubescens*.

A double gold lily, a white double may-weed and a meadow blue-bell.

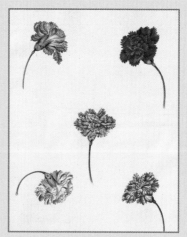

Five carnations, including General Tripoli, Belvedere, La Belle, Farie Hensen and Catrose(?).

A common red poppy, Jacob's Ladder and a corn cockle.

Two pink cabbage roses.

Narcissus radiiflorus, Narcissus poeticus, Fritillaria imperialis and two *Primula* x *pubescens*.

A Savoy spiderwort, two anemones and a crocus.

The great orange lily and a small bell-flower.

A sprig of arbutus with its fruit and two ducks in miniature pasted onto the page.

Double anemones, a hard-leafed anemone and an amaranthus.

A large double red peony and a large blush peony.

A Triumphant Jancussen carnation, the Prince of Wales carnation and a single sweet william of various colours.

A Province damask rose and a cats foot plant.

A white buttercup, a purple common milkwort and a striped tulip.

A small sunflower and a porcupine, rabbit, guinea-pig, two ducks and a goldfinch in miniature.

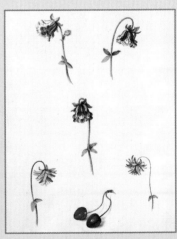

A Prince of Wales tulip, a Gedenelle tulip and a sprig of rosemary.

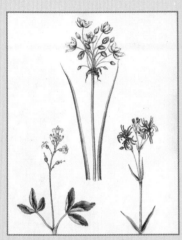

A wild ragged robin, a water gladiolus and a March trefoil.

The York and Lancaster rose, a field scabius and yellow jasmine.

Three hyacinths, a Persian iris, two Spanish daffodils and a purple crocus.

An Agatte tulip, a Penelope tulip and a yellow Crown tulip.

A striped tulip, a lily of the valley and a double wall-flower.

A tulip with red stripes and a striped leaf, a field pea and a sprig of Persian jasmine.

Two double purple-ringed daffodils, a single Gilli flower, an Agatte tulip and a Fine English tulip.

Five double columbines and two Duke cherries.

A Virginian martagon lily, a Virginian clematis, ivy-leaved sow-bread, cyclamens and a caterpillar.

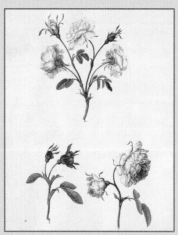

A white English rose, a Francfort rose and a Cinnamon rose.

Two Van Dewsport tulips, a black fritillary, a green anemone, a summer hyacinth and a ranunculus.

A branch of Rose of Holland and a piece of brook lime or blue water scorpion grass.

A passion flower, a sensitive plant, a cyclamen leaf and a chequered meadow saffron of Naples.

A variegated iris, a blue convolvulus, an upright willow-flower and a blue monkshood.

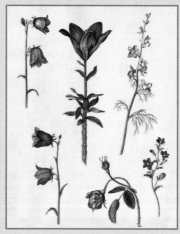

Two campanula, a sprig of rose-buds, an orange lily, pink larkspur and purple 'Venus Looking-glass'.

A white star of Naples, two grape-hyacinths, a variegated auricula and four variegated anemones.

Winter aconite, liverwort, twin-flowered crocus, crocus from Susa, Iran, a primrose, a dog and a bird.

A snowdrop, mezereon, a hyacinth, margined box, a spring snowflake, spring squill and two purple crocus.

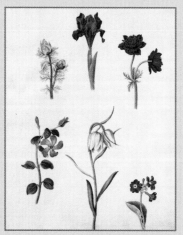

Ox-eye, dwarf-beared iris, poppy anemone, greater periwinkle, white snake's-head fritillary and auricula.

Fourteen auriculas (*Primula* x *pubescens*).

A ginger plant, two types of capsicum and a purple-leaved claire.

A scarlet coluthea, a blue cardinal flower and a bean caper.

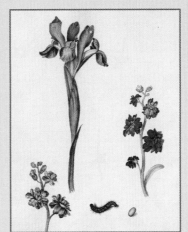

A variegated iris, two double stocks and a caterpillar and an egg.

A sprig of red currants, a sultan-flower and a St John's wort.

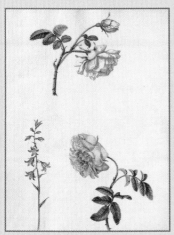

The white English rose, the double yellow rose and a sprig of small rampion.

A large sunflower and a greyhound in miniature.

Three carnations: La Princesse, Damasquin and the Red Admiral of Zealand and a bunch of Great Blue grapes.

Honeysuckle, a large blue lupin, a sprig of borage, 'Park Leaves' and a stag beetle, a fly, a grey monkey and a grey parrot in miniature.

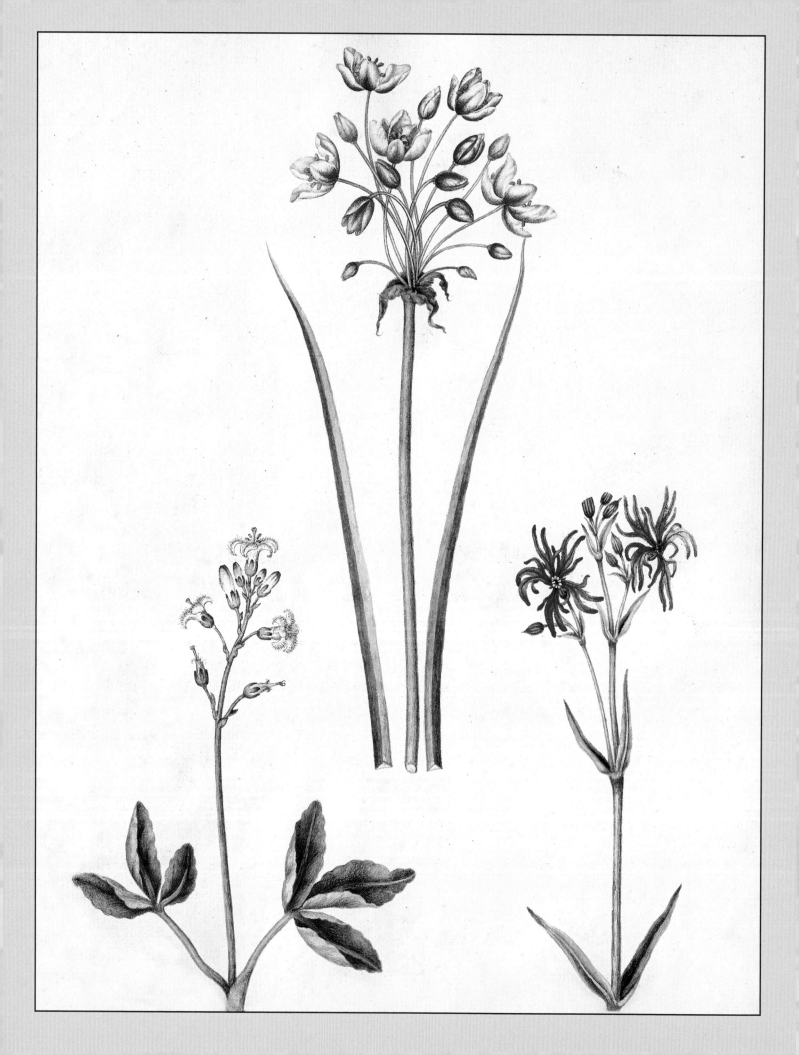

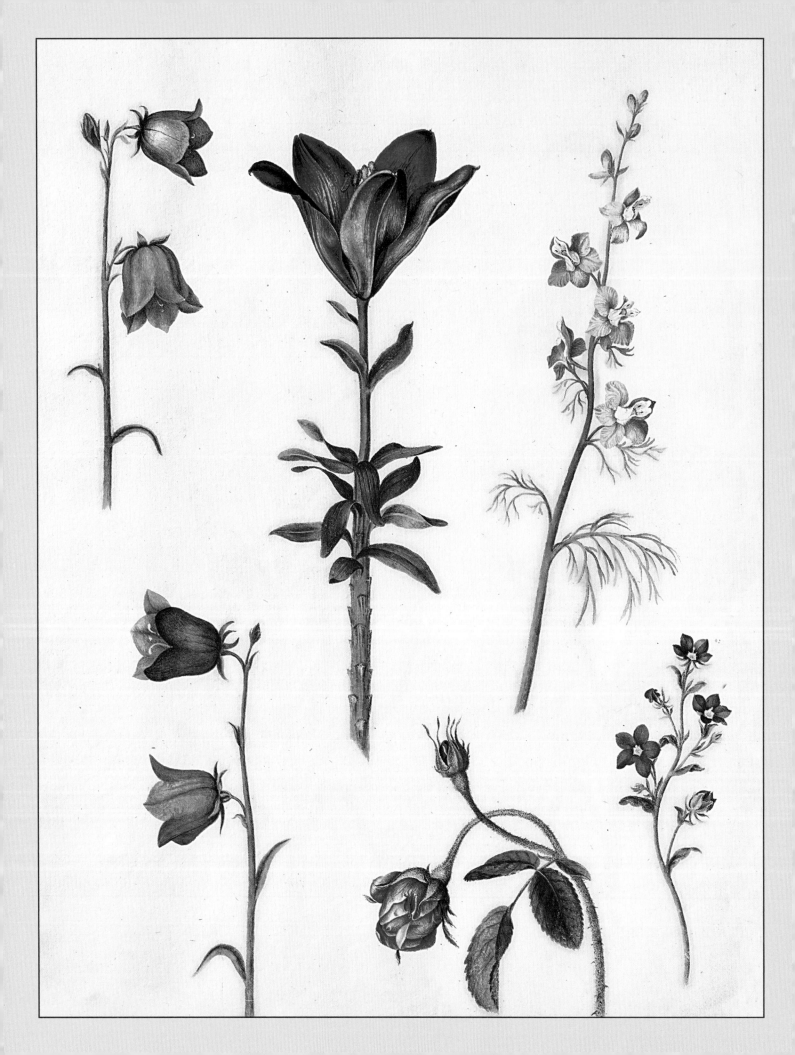

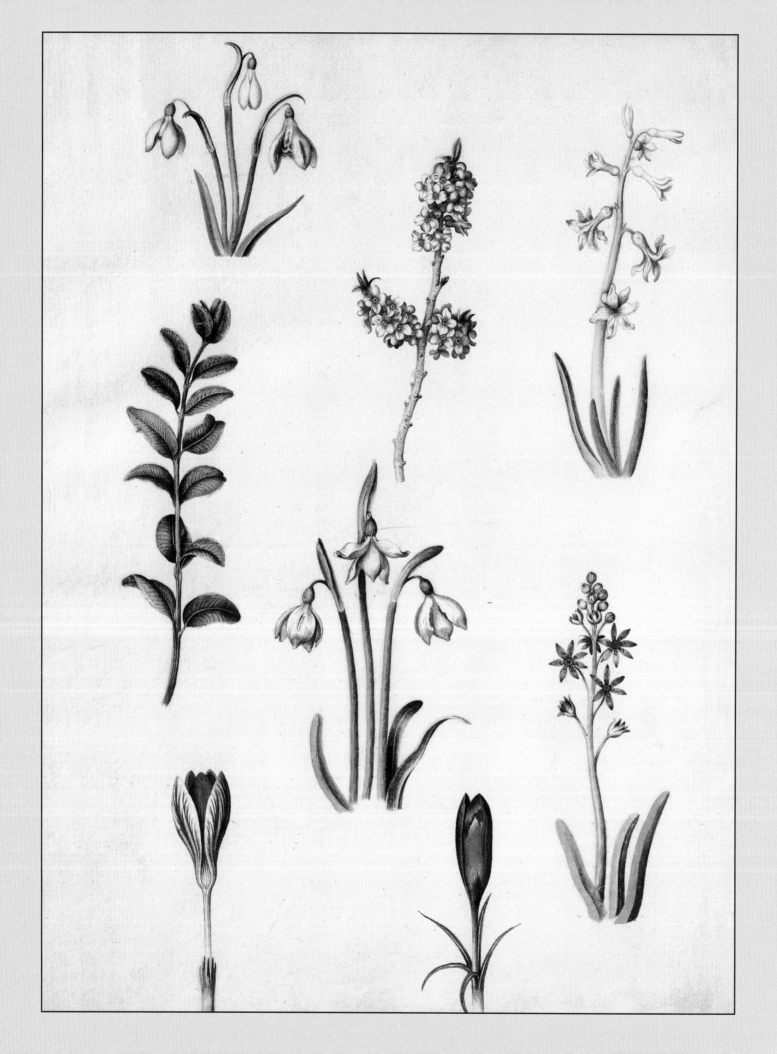

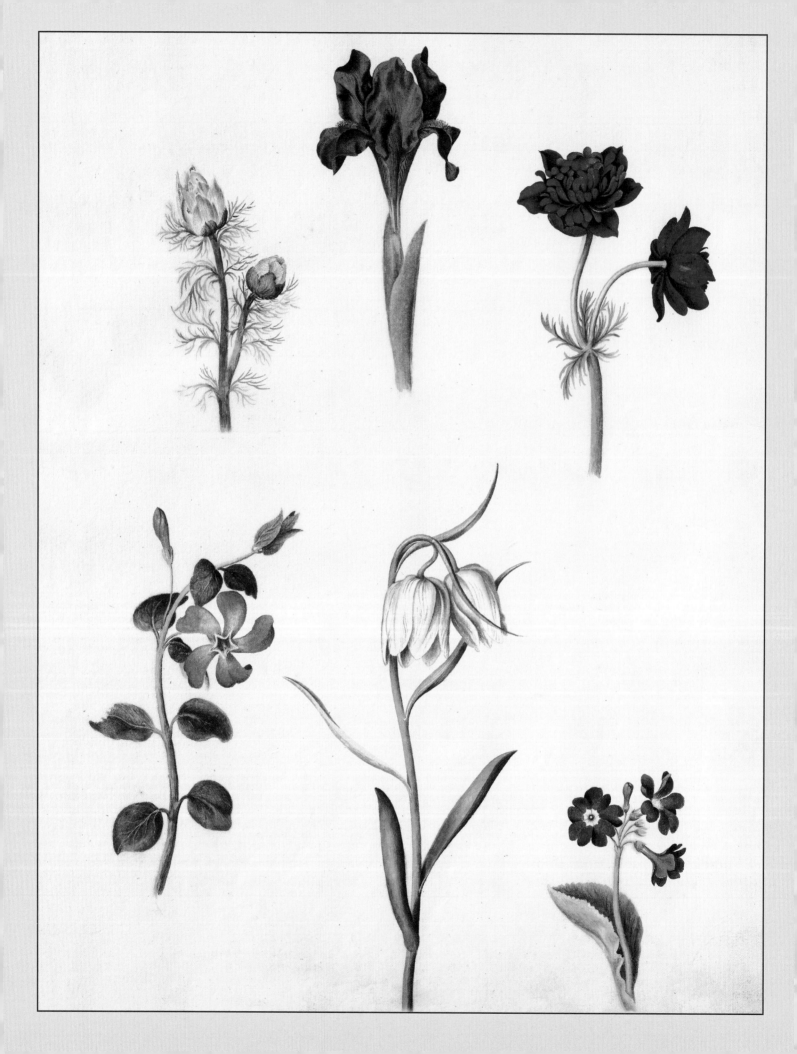

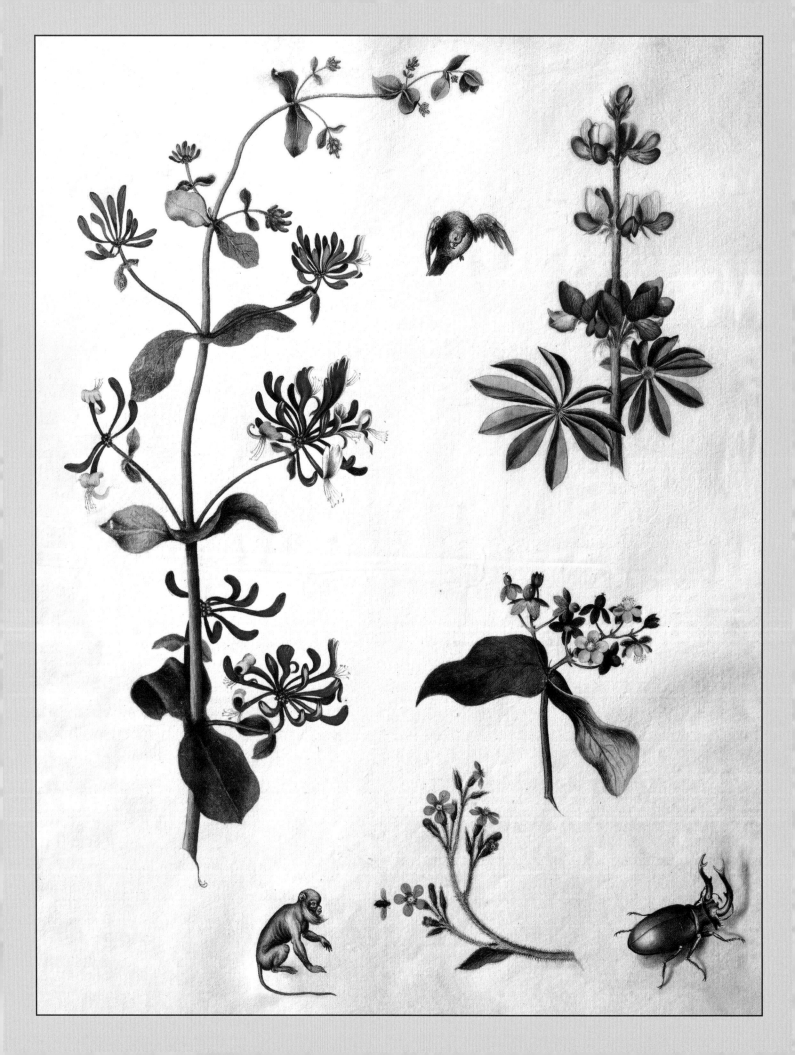